Make Him Beg and Get the Guy You Want

Choose, Tease, Ignore, Then... Catch Him!

The 4 Steps Foolproof Method on How to Attract Men and Make Them Obsessed With You

I0415431

JOSHUA CLETIS

CONTENTS

Introduction

Congratulations on downloading "**Make Him Beg and Get the Guy You Want Choose, Tease, Ignore, Then... Catch Him!**" I want to thank you for giving me a chance to share my knowledge on how to find the man of your dreams and make him fall in love with you. There's a ton of advice floating around on how to find a happy, satisfying relationship, but many women still find themselves at a loss. They date the wrong guys who don't appreciate them, they get ghosted sometimes, or their man simply does not treat them very well. If this sounds like you, it can end today by reading this book and following some of the expert advice given here.

This book contains the foolproof, four-step method on how to choose, tease, ignore, and catch a man. It covers topics such as insecurity, sex, boundaries, and physical attraction to equip you adequately in getting out there and finding Mr. Right. If you have been having trouble finding him, this book is for you. For as long as humans have been dating, they have been suffering from heartbreak and disappointment, often because no one ever shared the best dating tips with them. You're done with that life, though. It's time to take your future into your hands and find the relationship you deserve.

What you will gain inside this book?

- The four stages of making your dream guy yours (choose, tease, ignore, and catch)

- How to flirt like a pro and make him obsess over you

- The way men fall in love and what they seek in a female partner

- How to ensure that he stays interested and satisfied in your relationship once you do catch him

- Tips for texting him to keep the heat on even when you can't see him in person

- And so much more!

I hope you will enjoy this reading so to hear for your thoughts on Amazon.

Now get reading and join the party!

Chapter 1: A Brief Introduction on Why He's So Confusing

Hopefully, this isn't news to you, but men and women think differently usually. As a woman, you've probably gaped in confusion at a male friend getting into an argument at a bar or has gotten annoyed with your father for his habit of taking his shoes off in the living room and leaving them there, despite the fact that he is an otherwise organized person.

High school girls say it best: "Boys are so weird." This is totally true—why else would they spend money on expensive protein drinks but forgo nice little gifts to themselves like manicures and new t-shirts. Men are indeed weird sometimes, but there is more nuance to the statement than that. Men seem weird to women because they think differently from us, and we often don't know how to figure out what they're thinking and how they're sizing up a situation. Men actually think in some pretty consistent way, and knowing that can take a lot of stress out of our lives when it comes to understanding the male brain.

How Women Think

Hold on! Before you skip this section and tell me, "I'm a woman, of course, I know how I think," as you turn the page looking for the most interesting stuff, there is actually some important information in here. While, of course, you know yourself very well, you may not understand how that factors into being a woman. Understanding the ways women see the world will help explain how men see the world and how these perspectives are different.

Let's start with a simple little fact—women have a larger hippocampus than our male counterparts. The hippocampus is the part of the brain that regulates emotions, stores long-term memories, and helps with spatial navigation. Can you guess where this leads? It means that women can recall memories from long ago with richer detail and accuracy than a man. Women are also more likely to use landmarks to figure out where they are if they are lost, whereas a man will be more likely to try ascertaining the distance and direction he has traveled. These seem like somewhat irrelevant differences, but the point I'm trying to make is that there is an extremely compelling case, given our biology, that men and women do fundamentally process events and feelings differently, which influences how they make choices and relate to others.

Getting back to daily life outside the world of brain anatomy, you may have heard "women rely too much on their feelings to make decisions. They are highly emotional creatures." This is both true and untrue. Women are not incapable of logic critical thinking. Of course, we can do these things and do them well. But there is a grain of truth in this statement that actually is to the credit of the female gender. As a woman, when you are faced with a decision, you are probably much more likely to consider someone else's feelings when making a decision. You may make decisions based on the desire to spare yourself or others of any pain. This is not a bad thing—it is most likely the result of socialization. Women are often raised to be considerate of how others feel or to be on the defensive side of those who seek to do harm. Therefore, it is only natural that we grow up with a more diverse set of tools for decision making than men do—we use logic to get the job done right and sensitivity to make sure it all runs smoothly.

Another way women think differently from the men in their lives is that we are more likely to cooperate with others to solve a task than men are. Once again, this has a lot to do with how we are raised. Women are more likely to be brought up knowing it is okay to work with others; collaboration is often encouraged or even necessary to keep ourselves safe. We are generally less solitary and more social than men. We are more likely to engage in activities that facilitate chatting and sharing details of ourselves than men do. We generally think with the bigger picture in mind and are better at multitasking for the same reason. While men are commonly simply breadwinners and father figures, most women in today's society wear the hats of mother and worker while cleaning the house and maintaining a cohesive family unit. It only makes sense that women see the big picture more than men do in order to get all of these jobs done properly.

We also tend to be better at expressing ourselves verbally and have a better command of language than men. You know how you ask your man why he doesn't like something, and he responds, "I don't know; it's just ugly." In more intense situations, men often need to repeat themselves and have difficulty finding the words to talk about their feelings—they can't help it. Women's superior grasp of language may be a product of evolution. Over millions of years, women completed survival tasks that were more likely to be performed in groups and needed to be good communicators. As a result, women's brains evolved with the ability to choose words and learn languages with more facility than men.

Remember what I said about how women have better memories than men? We can quickly retrieve memories made long ago and get minute details right. In a disagreement, this is useful, but it explains another strange mismatch of the genders; women are more likely to use intuition to make a decision. Intuitive decision-making is a more useful strategy for women than it is for men because it innately requires long-term memory consolidation. Because women have a larger set of memories to influence decisions, we are more likely to think about a problem in general terms and take into consideration a lot of different factors when deciding what action to take. In a way, it's almost like we have more experience than men by having a more developed intuition—our richer memory consolidation gives us high-quality samples from the past to use to test our intuition in present situations.

How Exactly Do Men Think?

From experience, we all know that men have a different set of strengths and weaknesses than women. They perceive differently from us and often use different cognitive processes to solve problems. While screaming into a man's face, "WHY DID YOU DO THAT?!" may be necessary sometimes, knowing a bit before losing your cool may save you a lot of confusion when it comes to deciphering a man's actions.

One of the most common male behaviors that confuses us is taking a risk. I have found myself concerned when my father rides his bike without a helmet or when an ex-boyfriend told me he enjoyed going to casinos. Just hearing those stories made my blood pressure skyrocket at even the thought of taking chances like that. Although taking a risk often feels unpleasant and dangerous to women, men actually get a much bigger rush of endorphins from it than women do. Endorphins are the brain's feel-good chemicals that keep us coming back to sources of pleasure. Endorphins are one of evolution's best inventions. They kept our ancestors constantly seeking out rewards such as sex or food in order to ensure the continuation of the human race. The logical connection between risky male behavior and evolution is a little clearer now. Historically, men did the dangerous work of hunting for their communities and would always come back feeling victorious when they made the kill. In modern times, when most men do not risk their lives hunting down food, our pleasure-attuned brains still assert their wishes. Although men no longer hunt down all the community's food, the old system, where taking a risk provides pleasure, is still in place. Therefore, men often do not experience the anxious race of their hearts in a precarious situation as unpleasant. Rather, they draw strength and exhilaration from it.

A surprising rule that applies to most men is that they need wayyy more validation than they'll ever admit. Although men often seem as though they need approval from no one and act alone in all situations, men do not get as many compliments as women. Male friendships tend to be less conversational than women's, and they are less likely to complement each other. Most men enjoy a compliment from women, and in general, they are more likely to believe a compliment directed at them than women are. While a woman may assume a compliment toward her is flattery or generosity on the part of the person giving the compliment, a man will probably hear the compliment and feel very pleased with himself.

In addition, men are also more likely than women to fall for appearances. The saying "men are visual creatures" is a little bit strange—it's not just that men are visual creatures; it's more that they are more likely to take others at face value. Men are generally less analytical of other people than women are. This explains why men often fall for a pretty face and fail to see red flags about a woman's personality or other possible red flags. With that said, the fact that men are visual creatures who think more simply than women means that the male gaze is probably not as harsh on a woman as you may be toward yourself. A man is less likely to notice flyaway hairs or a small pimple than you think. In short, men do care about appearances, but they are not exacting and critical analyzers out to identify a woman's every flaw.

"What," "how," and "why," are probably three words you and a man do not have in common. Let me explain. As a woman, when you tell a story about going out with friends, you probably go in-depth about why something happened and divulge great detail about who said what, how the night went, and why things went down the way they did. A man, however, will often keep it short. He would describe the night something like this: "I went out for drinks. Had a good time. Beer." Men focus on what happened—the events themselves and not much else. On the other hand, women are more likely to focus on how and why. This difference in language often causes great frustration in heterosexual interactions of any kind. As women, we sometimes get annoyed by men's overly simplistic characterization of the world, and men often can't follow our analyses of events or even find them boring. This is neither a good nor a bad difference. It is simply that men often take in their surroundings, focusing on only one layer—the physical layer—while women take in two layers, which are the physical and its underpinnings.

In general, men also feel much more compelled to appear macho than women want to appear feminine. Men often adopt clothing (such as beards and camo in some places), and they work out to gain huge muscles. Often, they refuse to process or discuss their emotions. They also avoid stereotypically feminine activities all in the name of appearing manly. While, as a woman, you may feel comfortable ordering a whiskey at a bar or wearing a blazer without fear of being seen as too manly, men are often exceedingly anxious about not appearing overly feminine. This outlook informs much of what men do and how they behave. Be aware that men do this out of fear. They fear that they might lose the approval of their peers or be seen as girly (which many of them think is a bad thing, even though we know better). They fear being ridiculed or seen as weak. Most men are very protective of their masculine image of themselves, but with a little bit of coaxing and sensitivity from others, they can often be convinced to let their guard down a little bit.

What Do These Differences Mean to You

So, we know that men and women think very differently. This often causes friction and confusion in our relationships. Especially for women, a lack of understanding of how these differences affect us can make or break our relationships. The way we differ from men can introduce some serious difficulties when searching for a man.

One of the most common ways these differences affect our search for a good man, and probably the most important, is our distinct communication styles. Remember, "what, why, and how?" Those are back. Often, as women, we want our men to meet us exactly where we are with respect to transparency. Men, who often speak with less detail than women, may come off as though they are making a conscious effort to conceal information or be evasive. This is not the case, though. Men send out fewer hidden messages than women think. If a man you are interested in is not saying much, do not feel threatened or afraid. He is just thinking in his own terms, which often include fewer abstract ideas than yours.

Another obstacle that these differences present is that, given their riskier and more thrill-seeking ways, many men are afraid of commitment. Many men see settling down, and even exclusivity with a woman as giving up all of the fun and excitement life has to offer. While this is obviously wrong, knowing how much novelty excites men, it is unsurprising that many men feel this way when men avoid commitment but want a woman to stick around anyway. Of course, this creates a problem. Women seek security and consistency; we like closer relationships and are more socially adept, and commitment is a great place for these talents to shine through. When this opportunity is denied to us a by a man, it can create problems. A man may love your company, but still, he wants the company of other women and the excitement that something better (that they usually don't deserve) is just around the corner. As a woman, you don't really get what you want from this. You want a man who can commit and be reliable—not some man-child constantly chasing tail.

We can also be taken aback by masculine energy itself sometimes. While a lot of guys do go overboard, trying to prove how manly and tough they are, another important difference comes to mind, resulting from masculine energy. Men are better advocates for themselves than women are. Socialization often teaches men to be proud and even brag a little bit, while we learn early that "humble" equals "better." Throw this out the window. Do not be intimidated by a little bit of male bravado.

Another issue that causes friction between men and women is emotional unavailability. It may seem odd to think of this as a difference between men and women, but it is. Men and women are unavailable for different reasons. It goes back to commitment and security. Often, a man remains emotionally unavailable to a woman partially deliberately and partially on purpose—he is too busy looking for the next best thing, as we discussed earlier. Men view emotional availability practically as a symptom of commitment, so they stave it off. In addition, men are often inarticulate about their emotions and have difficulty with vulnerability. In this respect, emotional unavailability is a bit of an accident. Women go about this unavailability a little bit differently. Women are often like this on purpose, and with good reason. Most of us have met a guy who does not take us seriously, clearly is not looking for anything long term, or may just be a hot douche bag who is fun to pass the time with. We often know this is going on and preemptively protect ourselves by becoming emotionally unavailable.

The issue of emotional unavailability becomes frustrating because, at the end of the day, neither party usually likes being on the receiving end of obvious emotional distance. It often makes women feel disrespected or insecure that their fling does not really like them. A man, on the other hand, will feel a bit threatened when a woman is emotionally unavailable. He'll start thinking that she's hiding something, doesn't like him, or isn't giving him enough of her affection. To be clear, both genders actually have good reasons not to reveal everything to each other. It is a little bit of a coping mechanism—if someone does not share too much information with someone they're sleeping with, he or she can convince themselves that the social and sexual union didn't matter. As you may have suspected, this is kind of a shitty coping mechanism. It's the favorite drug of playboys and women hurt in the past, and it leaves both parties with a raging emotional hangover if they do it too much.

Here's the million-dollar question: where does this leave us? Confused. It lives in a town called "confused." Our GPS systems go haywire in it, and we lose our damn minds trying to figure it out. Because men and women see the world differently, attempting to make a connection with a member of the opposite sex can often feel like traffic in gridlock. So far, we know three common traps we fall into on this journey—overthinking, emotional burnout, and confusion. There is still a more insidious one, though. It creeps up on us, makes us eat ice cream in sorrow, and makes us bow our heads in shame. It makes us worry, spend money, and act clingy. Have you guessed what it is?

The Worst Consequence: Insecurity

Maybe you guessed it; maybe you didn't. Insecurity is often where our differences from men lead us. Before even introducing potential mates into the equation, many women are already insecure before the hunt begins. We all have had the moment where we think we look great until we look in a mirror and catch a bit of cellulite or a pimple. Sometimes, while we flip through a magazine and catch a model who is prettier, taller, and thinner than we'll ever feel, we go on to spend the next few hours feeling emotionally deflated and physically bloated. Other times, we feel as though we are never doing enough at work or not keeping our living space spotless enough. We feel not cool enough or not ANYTHING enough.

Romantic potential, especially if we are on the hunt for something long term, can often shift the spotlight onto insecurities we already have. When we start seeing a new guy or even just flirting with a new crush, all of our fears about ourselves can bubble up to the surface—"Does he even like me?", "Oh my God, he probably thinks I'm ugly," or "I can't text him first; that'll be so weird and then he'll think I'm inept and desperate, and I'll never leave my house ever again." The thought of rejection can often make us cower in fear like a shape-shifting boogie man able to embody all of our worst fears about ourselves. The only problem with this insecurity is that it has the potential of turning a man off and pushing him away.

Insecurity serves as a huge red flag to guys. When a man can smell the insecurity in a woman, he makes a few assumptions about her. While it may or may not be fair, the damage done by coming off as insecure is undeniable. To a man, insecurity suggests that a woman may be desperate, clingy, needy, or any other unattractive and attention-seeking quality.

You know the supply-and-demand curve. When the market gets flooded with an easily available product, people will pay less for it. If a brand becomes too ubiquitous, people get a little bit bored with it. Insecurity also works this way. One of the reasons it is such a huge turnoff to men is that it often makes a woman desperate and overly available. A good guy will not want someone who says "yes" constantly and chases affection. It makes a woman seem easy when she behaves desperately. A secure woman knows what she's worth and knows she does not have to do any chasing. Becoming a secure woman will prove to you that you don't need a man—you simply want a fabulous companion. Take this attitude wherever you go, and no guy will think you're desperate.

Insecurity can also make us jealous—anyone who has dated knows that jealousy is toxic. It brings out the worst in us, and, frankly, it makes someone an annoying person. No man meets an envious woman and fantasizes about having to insist to her eight thousand times that he was not, in fact, checking out her sister. It is annoying, and the accusations that a jealous person makes are often paranoid and an insult to the accused. With that said, it is hard not to be jealous sometimes, knowing that men are likely to seek out new women constantly and can be reluctant to commit. Jealousy, though, is often a little bit of a trick our mind plays on us. For example, you may be jealous of a woman because she is beautiful, but that jealousy blinds you to the reality of the rest of her life. Perhaps she is in an unhappy marriage. Maybe she is very insecure, or maybe her personality is boring. Jealousy can make us assume the worst about ourselves and the best about others; thinking like that is called cognitive distortion. Avoid jealousy by reminding yourself that you are unique, and that jealousy often warps our sense of reality.

A needy, weak woman who needs constant reassurance is usually tiresome as well. Of course, everyone has days where they don't feel themselves, but someone who constantly puts themselves down and needs to be showered in compliments is irritating. The types of men worth dating are perceptive that an insecure woman will be so paranoid that she will think of anything he does as a slight. The insecure woman constantly accuses her man of cheating or lying when he says he loves or likes her. This sort of behavior puts a guy on his guard. Do not constantly push him to "prove" his love. Try not to be the type of woman who obsesses over her man's ex-girlfriend or goes through his phone looking for betrayal. It is not only unattractive. It also harms you and drains your energy out of the fun you could be having.

With that said, you may be shaking your head at this page and thinking of many examples of hopelessly insecure women you know who are in relationships. It may be true that these women are in relationships, but men who date extremely insecure women often have insidious intentions. The man who wants a meek woman knows she can be easily manipulated and will not leave him because a breakup would be crushing to her self-esteem. Men who date insecure women are often cads and simply want someone they can hurt with no consequences.

The steps to finding a good man are: choose one, tease him, ignore him, and catch him. These steps have one preparatory step that comes before any of them—cultivating confidence. The confident woman is usually the sexiest in the room. She has a walk, a swagger, and a great story. The best of all? She gets the guy in the end. The woman who knows it is her God-given right to find a sexy, passionate, and kind man is the one who gets him. The woman who fears it will never happen for her is the one who settles out of loneliness and marries the first schmuck who seems marginally better than the other guys she has met. Ladies, you know what to do. Before choosing a man, be secure that you can score just about any guy out there.

Chapter 2: Eyes on the Prize— Choosing Who You Want

Have you ever bought a cool, new gadget only to take it home and realize it's useless and more of a pain than a blessing? Yeah, me too. A lot of women date this way, too. They meet a hot guy with whom there's reactive, fiery chemistry and begin a relationship full of volatile passion. He's hot, mysterious, and ever-so-slightly emotionally unavailable—there's always a lot of drama in these relationships.

All of the heightened emotions and lust of these relationships make us feel as though we have found a soulmate—"the one"—if you will call it. Well, that's the problem. If he's difficult and you constantly have to fight for his attention, affection, and respect, he is not actually the one. However, women often choose this type of guy because we believe that we can somehow convince him to commit to us. We chase and chase and chase but keep coming up empty-handed and out of breath from running after him.

We often fall for this guy because the serious and intense feelings we have as soon as we meet him are what love looks like but are really not. He keeps us on our toes, and we can never relax around him. It practically feels like a high when we see he sends a text or starts giving us the look. Herein lies the dilemma: feeling this heady and intense feels right , whereas going for the stable, reliable guy doesn't quite feel like an adrenaline-fueled joyride.

The healthiest relationships rarely start with uncontrollable passion and intensity, though. Healthy relationships start with a few interactions that are fun and pleasant without making you feel a nearly overstimulating headrush. You do not constantly check your phone to see if he has texted, and you don't feel the pull to check his social media pages obsessively. Instead, attraction with the nice guy grows slowly. We don't need to feel faint and anxious about a relationship with him constantly.

What Do You Want?

With all that said, maybe the exhilarating bad boy is what you want if you're in the mood for a summer fling or a fun hookup. Choosing the right guy involves doing some soul-searching about what you want at a given point in your life. By knowing whether you want a casual hookup or serious boyfriend (or something in between) and knowing which qualities in a man are important to you, you will have a much easier time finding a guy who fits the bill.

As you may suspect, this process starts with you. Figure out what your own values are in order to know who is compatible and what you will not compromise. For example, if you are someone who enjoys strict routines, such as working a nine-to-five job or keeping an extremely clean house, you probably value stability and order. It would be best for you then, to find a guy who also likes stability and order. He does not necessarily have to need these things in the exact same way you do, but such priorities should be as equally important to him as they are to you.

A big part of identifying what's most important to you is about what makes you happy and what grinds your gears. Maybe your most successful past relationships have been those where you and your man have a favorite activity in common. Maybe the guys you have all had healthy relationships with made you feel a certain way. On the flip side, ask yourself what your unsuccessful relationships had in common. Maybe it was lots of fighting, insecurity, jealousy, or infidelity. Knowing your own weaknesses and strengths, your likes and dislikes, and how all of those factors interact is a part of looking forward to a bright future with a sexy, kind man who knows how to treat you right.

This step is so important that you should write it on paper. Make a list of different things you want in relationships at different stages in your life. What did you want in high school? College? Mid-twenties? Take a look at how your taste has evolved over time, and also take note of what has remained mostly consistent. Take a look at the things that have stayed the same throughout your life because these are the qualities that are probably most important and non-negotiable to you.

Now that you know what you want, you're in a good place to start mingling and matching. Knowing what you want and what you absolutely can't stand will give you some insight into what your personal red flags are and what you are into. When you go out, keep the previous advice in mind. If he says something that sounds like it would annoy you terribly to live with or would make you morally uncomfortable, move on and find someone new.

Take a Step Outside of Yourself: Figuring Him Out

Picture this: you're at a bar, and a tall, dark, handsome stallion is chatting you up and giving you a smoldering stare. You sit there during the conversation and hear some stuff that sounds "weird" or makes your brow furrow a little bit. But he's so sexy and mysterious that you can ignore the tiny red flags pretty well. Everything seems to be going well, and he asks for your number, but you can't shake the feeling that something's off despite the magnetic chemistry between you two. Sometimes, we fall into a relationship with Mr. Red-Flag-Something's-Not-Right, and at the end of it, we're left wondering what went wrong or how we didn't notice all the disturbing little details about him adding up.

You can skip this whole overture by knowing what to ask yourself when you first meet a guy. It's easy to find a guy you think is cute and fun, but romance proves difficult when trying to ascertain what this dude's deal is.

1. **Is it easy to be around him?** The right guy isn't going to make you so nervous or self-conscious that you can't be yourself around him. Some jitters are, of course, normal and natural when you feel attraction and want to impress him, but they shouldn't be so bad that you end up hiding important parts of yourself for fear of driving him away. The guy you can be yourself with is the guy you want. Conversation flows easily, you laugh at the same things, and you are not constantly concerned that he secretly dislikes you.

2. **Do you feel secure around him?** This question sounds a little bit like the previous one, but it is an important component of getting along with someone. Feeling secure

around your potential man is how a healthy relationship starts. When you feel secure around a guy, you don't feel the need to defend your choices constantly or exaggerate how great you are. Security looks like having a peace of mind that he isn't playing you or that he'll probably call you again.

3. **Does it feel like the time you met a nasty ex-boyfriend?** If you're talking to a possible mate makes you feel the way meeting your ex did—whether it's over-the-moon crazy, bored, or anxious—reconsider your choice. Finding the right guy will feel different from the way meeting your exes did. To find a new guy who is right for you, you're going to need to feel some new things and try some new moves.

4. **Do you actually know anything about him?** This is a weird one; have you ever met a guy and talked for hours only to realize you left the conversation, knowing very little about him? Did something like this ever happen after going on a lot of dates? This is a red flag. A dude who obfuscates his life and practically refuses to talk about himself may be hiding something or maintaining emotional distance. Tread carefully in this territory. He may just be shy, but he could also be trying to keep secrets.

5. **Do you like him or what he does?** A

mistake that creeps up on many women is choosing a guy she doesn't actually like. This sounds obvious, but it's actually pretty easy to fall into a relationship with a dude we don't actually like. This happens when, for example, a guy constantly compliments us. Everyone likes compliments, but often, if a dude lavishes us with them nonstop, we may wind up falling in love with the validation and not the guy. The same goes for forcing ourselves to date the guy who's great on paper. Maybe he does have a great job, swanky apartment, no debt, and no kids—but if you just don't feel secure around him or find yourself bored or annoyed, it doesn't really matter that he checks all the boxes.

Knowing that you actually like this guy and that he isn't shady is only part of the equation though. These qualities are merely the bare minimum of what the right guy will have. He, too, should have some qualities that entice you and make him reliable and considerate. An ideal dude will have a few traits that keep you simultaneously excited and calm, in love and independent, and impassioned but rational.

One of the first signs of a good guy is that he is a gentleman. He may exhibit classic gestures like pulling out your chair, but he may also exhibit this more subtly. A gentleman acts on the principles of politeness and consideration. A gentleman will not

invite you over for Netflix and chill on a first date—
he is not expecting sex as soon as he meets a woman.
Gentlemanly behavior may sound a little bit clichéd
or outdated, but it is an important step in figuring
out whether your guy cares about you as a woman. If
he acts inappropriately on a first date—drinking too
much, asking intimate and rude questions, etc.—
he'll only get worse as you get to know him.

The man you want also has integrity. Having
integrity means he's honest, sticks to his word, and
is morally upright. It's a component of healthy pride.
When a man has integrity, not only does he act on
principle and morality, but he also does these things
for himself. He isn't just nice to impress others; he
does not put in hard work solely to impress his boss.
He behaves this way because it's the right thing to
do, plain and simple. Integrity means he doesn't cut
corners or behave slyly. He's direct and does not see
any reason to cheat in order to get what he wants.

Another important quality is maturity. While party-
boy, who also loves his video games, may be super
fun don't be surprised if his childlike side comes out
in not-so-cute ways. The immature man will pick
fights over silly disagreements, give you the silent
treatment, and be uncompromising. Emotionally
mature men, however, will be able to express their
disagreement calmly and will not resort to low blows
to get what they want.

What makes it so hard to find the right guy is often
our personal baggage. Countless women have had

absent or abusive fathers, for example, only to find themselves dating similar men in the future. When women realize the similarity, they become rightly horrified. This happens for a reason, though. Subconsciously, they're trying to revisit the scene of the crime and somehow correct a painful past. If a woman could not get her father to express his love for her adequately, she may turn to men similar to him in hopes of proving to herself that she is worthy of the love her father could not provide her. This can happen in other ways, too. Maybe you've always been insecure about your looks, so when you meet a man who acts as if you're the sexiest thing on earth, you glom on like a barnacle. Maybe you like to be perceived as highly successful, so you keep dating men so invested in their careers that they are serious workaholics. To put it concisely, make sure you are choosing men using your strengths and not your weaknesses.

Now that you know what to consider when choosing the right guy, it's all a strategy game. Have you ever played chess? It requires planning, cunning, and a little bit of risk-taking. It also requires knowing your opponent. Although you may have the guy chosen by now, assessing his intentions is the next big step. Once you zero in on your hottie, make sure he's after the same thing you are. Nothing is worse than sleeping with a guy and going on some dates only to realize he views you as a casual fling while you're out looking for a husband.

You Know What You Want…But What About Him?

Meeting a great guy is, well, great. He's nice, the sex is great, and the conversation is witty and fun. One little detail keeps nagging at you, though—you can't quite figure out what he wants. Somehow, you guys have been having sex and going on dates for THREE BLISSFUL MONTHS, but he seems a little bit dodgy about the question, "what are we?". The good news is that there are some subtle hints he'll drop to let you know about his headspace. By understanding how to decipher his language, you can get a pretty clear picture of where the relationship is going before you even ask him.

Let's start with the worst-case scenario first—he really likes you but isn't looking for more than a hookup. If he's only looking for sex, do not expect a good-morning text or an after-work text, asking how your day went. The dude who is looking only to get laid will most likely keep the texting to nighttime. If he texts at night, he's looking to see whether he can ask you to come over or to get his flirt on. In addition, if he never asks about how you're doing or what you're up to, there's a good chance the relationship he wants is only physical.

Another sign of Mr. Hit-it-and-quit-it is if he asks you to come over to his place without ever having spent any time with you outside on a real date. So if he's asking you to come over and "watch a movie" or have a drink, there's a good chance that no movies will be watched. If you're looking for a more serious relationship, think twice about getting involved with a guy who can't be bothered to leave his place to see you.

Your new boo may also not take you too seriously if he enjoys playing head games with you. If you wind up having to make all the first moves and he's not super enthusiastic to talk to you or get to know you, he is not very interested in you as a person. Making you do all the work is because he doesn't think you're worth the effort and is trying to calculate whether you will give it up after a couple of dates or even on the first night.

Now that you know the tell-tale signs that he doesn't want a relationship, we can turn toward figuring out whether he does want more commitment. This section is all about how he'll go out of his way for you or how much energy he's willing to spend without getting any sex in return. A good rule of thumb in finding out how much commitment a guy wants is how much he shows you unsolicited kindness and consideration.

Consideration is not just being attentive to your needs—at its base level, think a little more literally—does he ever think about you in a way that does not include the end goal of sex? The answer is yes if he texts you good morning, for example. Another way he may show you're important is by offering to do you a favor. Maybe you're moving soon or have come down with a cold. Hearing you're putting up with something difficult will send him into a boyfriend mode if he's into you but you're not yet in a relationship. Look for signs that he's thinking about you when it's not just about sex, like when he's sober or when he shows you a silly meme in the middle of the day.

He is also probably thinking about you seriously if he brings you around his friends. A guy who has boxed you into the hookup category will want to keep you there—away from the rest of his life. If he wants you to get to know his friends and you're getting to know all of them, it's because he wants you to be a part of his world. Introducing you to his friends and acclimating you into his clique shows that he wants you in a part of his life that is bigger than just his bedroom.

A guy who is looking for a relationship will also be down to hang out, even if you're not DTF. The fact that he's alright just watching television or getting a slice of pizza means he actually enjoys your company. This sign is especially important; if he is not looking only for sex, he actually gives a damn about getting to know you. It may seem a little bit strange that if he likes you, he won't want to jump immediately to sex, but it makes sense. If a guy is alright holding off or simply not looking to hook up every time you guys hang out, that means he sees you as more than just a woman to help him get his rocks off. He sees you as a good companion and likes qualities about you other than your body.

Last but not least, he actually cares about your thoughts and opinions. If he wants something more, he wants to hear about your thoughts and opinions and is not afraid to have some healthy debate with you. A guy who only wants to get in your pants will be as charming and smooth as possible to ensure an, er, easy entry. Men who are open to share ideas want a physical and intellectual connection. A guy who wants to commit is a guy who wants to communicate.

So He Wants to Commit—What Could Go Wrong?

Hold on there, baby! It's great that he wants to commit. That's fabulous, actually! But don't go straight for the first guy who wants a girlfriend. You're not looking to settle, babe. There is a chance that he's the needy or desperate one. Make sure this isn't the case. Your choice is important, and a bright future depends on making good dating choices.

One of the first good-guy red flags that there may be trouble lurking beneath the surface is that he is gratuitously into PDA. After a certain age, making out in public is rude and weird. It's a practice usually reserved for the drunk and disorderly. If he's constantly groping your ass in public or making a point to be all over you, reconsider committing to him. He may be super enthusiastic and unable to keep his hands off you, but he may also need constant reassurance of your attraction to him or be overly possessive. It's not an automatic disqualifier, but be aware that constant PDA gives an insight into his attitudes about you and the relationship.

An overly needy guy will also have no friends other than you. Okay, maybe he'll have a few, but it seems like he wants to spend absolutely all of his time with you. This could also be a sign that he's desperate. A guy who is lonely, bored, or both may start craving romance like a drug and want to use it all the time. Not only can this get annoying, but spending all of your time with a significant other is also unhealthy for both partners. A guy with no life outside of your time with each other is usually a guy with nothing to talk about, and he may even get angry if you have plans besides seeing him. He may get annoyed if you go out with friends without him or do not feel like accompanying him to an activity you don't particularly enjoy. Needy or desperate guys often lack boundaries, and not respecting your alone time is a good indicator that he doesn't respect your personal space.

You should also be a little bit wary of a guy who seems nice but won't stop blowing up your phone throughout the day. This can be a sign of many problems with him, but most importantly, it is super annoying to the recipient of the barrage of text messages. If your chosen man constantly texts you, it may mean he has nothing better to do; he's needy, doesn't respect your boundaries, and is overly aggressive. A guy doing this probably does not mean to bug you, but he should still know better than to bug you so much.

To be fair, none of these infractions are so huge— that's not what I'm saying at all. Rather, this section is a little reminder that not all that glitters is gold. He may seem super nice and ready to commit, but think a little bit hard if he seems needy or unable to leave you alone. These aren't necessarily deal-breakers, but they are qualities to be aware of before agreeing to a relationship.

Why We Often Have Problems Choosing the Right Guy

It's hard, I know. You often have to wade through a sea of Mr. Wrongs to find Mr. Right. Along the way, most of us date some men we're not all that into, who are not into us, and who are straight up terrible. Often, when we see a friend dating a total whack job, we gossip and ask, "what does she see in him?" Take a walk down memory lane, and you'll probably find yourself asking that same question about yourself.

Everyone makes mistakes, but they say a lot about us. We often make romantic choices based on what's missing in our own lives or on our past experience. Women go with what feels right, and often, our unconscious insistence on repeating past mistakes leaves us with a subpar dude who doesn't treat us right.

To start from the beginning, look back to your childhood. Do you see it clearly? Now, look at the guys you've dated. If you've always dated bad boys and troubled lads, your family may play a part in this. Women who grew up in difficult households—maybe having a loved one with an illness or substance abuse problem—often date similarly troubled men in an unconscious effort to revisit the past. We know we can't literally go back, but perhaps in "fixing" a broken guy, we can somehow correct the past. This never works. As wonderful a girlfriend you may be, a man cannot become a better person through love alone. In particular, a difficult father figure may cause a woman to choose the wrong guys later in life. As women, our fathers are our first male love. Dads teach their daughters by example on how they should expect to be treated by a man. If a father has abandoned his daughter or is emotionally, physically, or sexually abusive, a daughter will learn from this. The same is true if he's emotionally unavailable or absent and if he treats his daughters' mother badly. Take a look at your past to see if you keep repeating your relationship with your dad in your adult romantic relationships. Is there a pattern?

Low self-esteem is a major saboteur of your choices in men. If you have low self-esteem, you probably believe some pretty nasty things about yourself. "I'm not good enough for anyone to really like me" or "why would anyone love me if I'm not pretty, thin, smart, or accomplished?" Maybe your low self-esteem manifests as a negative outlook on love and life. Often times, these thorns in our psyche steer us toward choosing the wrong boyfriend because something about these men or our relationships with them confirms our view of the world or ourselves. It goes back to familiarity—if a partner who is otherwise bad for us makes us feel correct in our pessimism and low self-esteem, we are not intellectually challenged. Remember that saying, "better the devil I know than the devil I don't?" A lot of women actually live by that and would rather be with a man who exhibits douche-bag behavior that they're familiar with than take a chance on a guy who is not normally their taste.

Be wary of only dating guys who are your "type," especially if you seem to have a problem in dating jerks. Stepping out of your comfort zone may be the best decision you ever make. If you grew up in a house where parents constantly fought, then maybe you assume that normal relationships include constant fighting. Maybe dad stayed out late constantly without telling anyone when he would return, so you also internalized this as acceptable behavior. The problem with settling for volatile, dramatic relationships is that they become addictive. Spending some time with a nice guy may seem boring at first, but if you guys hit it off, it will have all the fun of your previous relationships without the constant stress. If a relationship with a particular type of guy you have been choosing before has not worked out, it may be time to try something new.

What Different Dudes Think About When Choosing You

As you may have suspected, not all guys want the same things out of a partner or relationship. This often depends on how old the guy is and what his life circumstances are. Depending on his age, he may have all sorts of variable expectations and desires.

The youngest age that most of us start dating is in our teenage years. Usually, a guy from high school or an extracurricular activity becomes our first boyfriends. They are often our classmates, neighbors, and friends. First boyfriends are also usually stressful as hell! With all those hormones racing, teenagers often can't figure out what they want, who they want, and how to go about getting it. If you're a teenage girl reading this, it's good to be aware of what your possible new squeeze may be looking for in a girlfriend.

An obvious answer to the question of what the adolescent male is looking for is sex. Don't think that's all there is, though. Teenage boys have other interests, too, and are often just as scared and confused as their female counterparts. Teenage boys are mostly looking for someone fun to hang out with and to whom they are immediately physically attracted to—that's why crushes are such a big deal in high school.

High school boys place a lot of emphasis on chemistry. It means that if conversations in-person or over text fall flat, they'll probably move on. Teenage boys also want someone they can hang out with; they probably aren't looking to take you on expensive dates, but they do think it's important that going on drives and watching television with you is a good time. This is a good thing, though! If you, too, focus on finding a guy you enjoy doing nothing with, you are more likely to find a guy you can get along well.

Lots of high school boys also want more emotional support than conventional wisdom suggests. Boys often hide their feelings from their friends for fear of teasing or because of the incessant competition among boys. A lot of young men, when they finally meet a girl they like, feel a great deal of relief upon acquisition of a love interest. As his girlfriend, you are under no obligation to be his therapist, but keep in mind that he probably has more complicated emotions than the world gives him credit for. Hear him out, and listen to him the way you would listen to a female friend.

Later in life, guys become a little more complex. In late adolescence into their mid-twenties, most guys are not looking for relationships. Like women, they are busy building careers and enjoying the freedoms of their new status as adults. With that said, a lot of guys' entry into adulthood and away from the prying eyes of parents gives them the freedom to pursue relationships their parents would not approve of in high school. A lot of men of this age who are open to relationships also just ended their awkward phase—

they shot up a few inches, their skin cleared, and they started dressing a little better.

Newly minted adult males are often looking for fun and spontaneity in a girlfriend. Our late teens and early twenties are often full of partying, studying, traveling, job hunting, and a whole slew of novel experiences. Guys want a sexy partner to share these firsts with and who can stay up all night talking but also know how to have a little fun.

Guys of this age also have a little bravado. This means that they do consider physical attractiveness high on the list of priorities and may be interested in engaging in some PDA to show off to friends. He may also play a little bit hard to get while you're first getting to know each other and may need a bit of ego-stroking to get the ball rolling toward a relationship. In the same vein, the boys in this age bracket may be a little bit insecure. They often do not want to know all about your past relationships and prefer to think they are the only man in your life. If you can, play along with this a little bit so long as it is not too ridiculous or demanding. Guys of this age are fun and usually emotional baggage-free. Take advantage of this—you will never be as free as you are at this age.

The adult male has even more exacting tastes than the young stallion, but the good news is that the fully grown adult male older than twenty-seven is usually a little bit less superficial than his younger brothers. By this age, most guys are settled in their careers and looking to settle down.

What characterizes a grown man is his focus on purpose. By this age, men are certainly still down to have some fun with a girlfriend, but they are not necessarily looking for the life of the party. This guy is looking for someone to take home to mom. He wants a responsible woman with family values and a sense of direction in life. At this age, it becomes clear to both men and women that a pretty face and a lot of fun do not make a relationship. This guy is looking for the package—he wants a woman with a steady job, a life of her own, and a formed personality.

In adulthood, guys are not as excited by the game playing and awkwardness that makes high school and college flirtations so exciting. He wants to talk through everything instead of awkwardly skirting around issues and places greater emphasis on emotional intimacy. Once again, guys of this age are usually looking to settle down. They are actually aware now of what they want in a partner. At this step, being an authentic and great version of you is important. No man will want a woman without interests, hobbies, and a whole life outside of dating. He also does not want a woman who acts ingenuously solely to find a man.

Later in life, if you are still single, divorced, or widowed, you may find yourself dating a mature man. This is the silver fox. Maybe he's been divorced and has some adult children. The older man will have the highest standards of all the age brackets when it comes to dating. By forty-five, most guys have seen it all.

An older man is interested in boundaries and will not tolerate red flags or serious flaws. At this age, men are not simply looking to dilly dally. A younger man may have a thing for an outgoing personality, and great sex is the most important thing a girlfriend can give. But an older man will be more exacting. He's looking for someone honest and real. Men of this age do not want immaturity or passive-aggression.

At this age, honesty is so important because most men have some baggage, like an ex-wife or children to take care of, and they know that a partner will most likely have something similar. By forty, most people have an entire life behind them; they are less of a blank slate. Therefore, older men value honesty because it allows a clear picture of your previous life and what sort of baggage you may bring to the relationship. If you are dating an older man, make sure he is honest about his own baggage as well. No adult wants to waste time and find out important details about a partner well into the relationship.

The silver fox also wants a self-assured woman by his side. At this age, codependency is not cute. Younger people want to build a life and future together, but after forty-five, two adults are looking to share worlds that already exist fully formed, unlike younger people who are still in the construction phase of adulthood. This means that the mature man wants a woman who knows who she is and brings some of her own ingredients to a relationship. His deal woman will be down for some new experiences and adventures and also assured of what she likes and dislikes. The mature man does not want a wishy-washy woman who responds, "Oh, I don't care where we go," when he asks where they ought to go to dinner. In short, the older man wants you to be your own person.

Choosing a guy can be hard. There are many options that look promising but prove to be Trojan horses. The good news is that you know what to watch out for and how to figure out what you want. In the next chapter, we can look into the different types of men out there in further detail. The next chapter will cover relationships with an age gap, younger men, and men who are already engaged. All of us want to wind up with our first choice, and knowing how to get the guy, depending on his precise place in life, will save you a lot of time and disappointment.

Chapter 3: It's Raining Men (Of All Types!): How to Choose the Right Man

You already know how to choose a man, but sometimes, your taste may be a little bit more demanding. Sometimes, we are dealing with some unusual circumstance or have a very specific sort of relationship in mind. The advice in the previous chapter was a more general guide, but here, we will take a deeper dive into some men who are a little bit harder to catch. In this chapter, I'll cover attraction and managing a mixed-age relationship, dating younger men, sugar daddies, and even men already in relationships!

Enticing the Older Man

So, you want an older guy. You've probably seen relationships with a young woman and an older, successful male and wanted to be that woman sometimes. Good for you! Contrary to popular belief, this relationship is actually empowering to both parties. Relationships like these are often satisfying and fulfilling to the older man and the younger woman because they require lots of communication to make sure everything goes smoothly and because both partners are often acutely aware of what their counterpart needs.

When an older man is looking for a younger woman, it's usually because he knows exactly what he wants and has trouble finding it in women his own age. Aside from beauty and youth, what a young woman can really offer an older man is her attitude. What the mature gentlemen see in a younger partner is her outlook on life—she's usually not so jaded and willing to have lots of carefree fun, unlike women older than herself.

One of the most important qualities an older man wants in a younger woman is admiration. That's not to say he wants undying sycophancy, but he's definitely looking for some appreciation from you, his new squeeze. The mature man is often further along in his career and fairly accomplished. He's looking for a lady who appreciates that about him and looks up to him. This guy, in addition to being fun, also wants to be sort of a mentor and provider for you. Younger women often fit the bill for this type of older man because they are more open to being taught. Older women have often learned life lessons on their own and are not open to the concept of looking up to their man for guidance and advice. A man who does want to share his knowledge and expertise may want a younger woman then. If this sounds appealing, too, you're in it for the right reasons.

Don't think dating an older guy is all about learning, though. There's certainly a lot of fun to be had. A lot of men looking for younger female partners are looking for the excitement and adventure not often found in older women. They want a woman who can stay out all night with them and make them feel young again. Relationships with older men are often filled with fun and novelty. An older man usually seeks to share his accumulated wealth with someone who will appreciate his accomplishments and add excitement to his life he may not have had as a younger man.

In order to attract this man, you have to be a particular type of package. The first step is actually displaying some maturity. Do not start seeing an older man only to become wishy-washy about the relationship. Mature men had already dated when they were younger and experienced the guessing games that frequently come with the youth dating scene. They're over it. Be direct, straightforward, and self-confident the way a mature woman often is. An older guy will appreciate someone who can keep up with him with respect to emotional intelligence. Not embodying the typical immaturity that often comes with young adulthood will do you a great deal of good in getting on an older man's good side.

In addition, invest some in your physical appearance. I am not going to lie to you and say an older man is attracted only to a youthful personality—the look is certainly important, too. Invest in a gym membership and a good haircut, and dress with some glamor. The key here is sexy elegance. An older man certainly wants a sexy little minx, but not one that dresses like a club rat. So, when dressing for an older man, do not choose your tiniest denim skirt and your most cleavage-bearing top. Instead, try something like dark jeans and a tight top with sexy but not over-the-top makeup. Remember, the mature man wants a woman he can look classy with and who compliments the fact that he has aged like a fine wine.

This goes without saying, but in case it isn't obvious, do NOT pursue an older gentleman only for his money and place all of your affection toward his bank account. Older men who date younger women are already aware that some of their female suitors are more interested in their income than them. An older man will appreciate that you accept him as a complete human being. Of course, you can appreciate some of the material benefits of dating someone older, but do not make the whole relationship about the vacations and jewelry you can get out of him. This is a boyfriend, not a piggy bank.

Another obvious tip you may miss is: flirt with the guy, for god's sake! To attract an older man, it will help make the first move (as it will in many romantic situations). With that said, you can't quite flirt with an older man the way you would with one of your peers. When flirting with the silver fox, don't be afraid to acknowledge the age gap. It's obvious to both of you, and having a fun attitude about him will make everyone breathe a sigh of relief. You also should work some flirtation into asking him for advice. Since he's older, he's been there and done that (whatever it is) and would be happy to answer your questions. Did you know that you've flirted with a guy your own age when you asked him to help you move apartments or get a work project done? The same strategy applies to the older man. Work some flirtation into otherwise normal conversations while stroking his ego by acknowledging that he has a thing or two to teach you about.

Dating the Older Man

Congratulations! All your flirting and grooming have finally attracted your real-life George Clooney. I must say, I'm proud. There's still more to learn, though. Dating an older man has some key differences from dating a man the same age as you. The care and maintenance of an age gap relationship can be tough, but it's so worth it.

When you first start dating your more advanced boo, you have to accept his past baggage if you want to be with him. After a certain age, everyone has had their fair share of past relationships. Maybe he has an ex-wife or children; maybe he has been through some trauma. Having more years than you means he has probably seen more of the world than you. As a younger woman, you are more of a blank slate then he is. Given his circumstances, you must accept the obligations he has to the life he had before his relationship with you. You also need to accept his emotional baggage. Having lived a longer life than you, he may have a sick parent or past relationships which haunt him. That's totally okay—everyone eventually accumulates their fair share of battle scars as life progresses. But be aware that he may have more than you and that you must support him as he maintains his life, such as caring for his children or paying child support to an ex.

Another important part of dating an older man is respecting his preferences and knowing when he is open to having his mind changed. Once again, he's been around longer than you have—he's probably more set in his ways than you are. This does not mean deferring to him about all decisions and pandering to all of his opinions. If changing his mind about something is very important, by all means, take a shot at it. On topics such as a living arrangement or in areas related to convention and tradition, be prepared for some stubbornness on his part. In these areas, respect his opinion. This is an extension of appreciating the age gap. He is most likely set in a lot of his ways because he has the wisdom to know what works and what doesn't. Learn to be alright with this; be happy that some of the reason he may not be so open to change is that he has had more years than you to practice some trial and error.

When entering this relationship, think in his age the way you switch languages in your head (if you're bilingual). Think about the years ahead when dating this guy. Would he want kids in ten years? Does he want to buy a house now instead of later or regret not buying it earlier? If the age gap is extreme, you may need to be prepared to take care of his health in a way you would not need to in a relationship with someone of the same age. Thinking toward the future means that you are considerate of his needs as an older gentleman, the same way he ought to be considerate of some of your needs as a younger woman.

Let's Turn Back Time: Dating a Younger Man

On the flip side, you may be attracted to a younger guy—making you a sexy cougar! Wear this badge with pride. Women who date younger guys are usually sexy, vibrant, and experienced. They know what they want. Men who date older women also have exacting tastes. They crave a few things that are hard to find in a girl their own age, and you, an older woman, may have just what it takes to captivate this boy.

Older women, like older men, attract younger

guys because of their experience and confidence. When a young man pursues a relationship with an older woman, it means he is enthralled by the woman's appeal in many ways. The most obvious one is her sexual experience. Older women often have fewer sexual hang-ups and less shame than younger women, and men of all ages tend to like this quite a bit. An older woman's experience also makes her a better flirt most of the time because she has most likely been in enough relationships to know that coyly twirling her hair simply isn't going to cut it to get everything she wants.

Perspective also plays a huge part in a man's chase for a cougar. An older woman can often offer her younger boyfriend a vantage point he never considered. This comes down to experience too. An older woman often shows a young man what it's like to date a sexy, mature, and self-confident woman. Many young men have not experienced any of those three characteristics from a previous girlfriend, and meeting someone who possesses those qualities is exceptionally alluring. An older woman also offers a pretty laid-back attitude about romance, which may be a breath of fresh air for the boy who has only been with his young, neurotic female peers. An older woman has done a lot of dating most likely—she knows that dating itself is supposed to be fun and enjoyable. A younger guy will appreciate someone who is not constantly asking, "what are we?" and "do I look fat in this?"

A younger guy will also appreciate how level-headed and calm an older woman can be. Younger women often want to party it up every weekend and get rowdy while an older woman may enjoy more low-key environments. A young guy who doesn't like hectic environments will enjoy that his older woman would rather hang out in an art gallery or a wine bar than at a loud night club.

The key to making a relationship like this work is to acknowledge the age gap without emasculating or mothering your boy toy. He enjoys that you are older, but he does not want to be dating his dowdy, domestic mother. Treat him as an equal and be open to his immature side. This relationship depends on playing up your similar interests (such as low-key venues and sexual exploration) while acknowledging and respecting the differences between you two.

Now For Dessert!

Do you know what a sugar daddy is? If you have a sweet tooth, this relationship may be for you. In case you haven't heard, a sugar daddy is usually a wealthy, accomplished man who takes care of a younger woman materially and financially in return for her companionship. Sugar dating includes all types of perks for both parties and can result in a mutually beneficial relationship for the sugar daddy and his sugar baby.

Sugar dating can be a long-term commitment

where the sugar baby receives a monthly allowance, or it can be a pay-per meet arrangement where the sugar daddy pays his girl each time they spend together. Contrary to popular belief, sugar dating is simply and absolutely not prostitution. While a sugar daddy and his sugar baby do have sex in most relationships, a sugar daddy is not just paying for the opportunity to lay a beautiful woman. Rather, he is paying for her companionship—they go on dates, have fun together, and develop a friendly and fun relationship. Some sugaring relationships even end in marriage! In return for his generosity, a sugar baby often offers her man a youthful escape from life and the opportunity to date a younger woman without any serious commitment like marriage or serious emotional conversations and fights typical of more traditional romantic relationships.

To be a sugar baby, you need to be beautiful and invest in your appearance. What helps is putting yourself out there by joining websites like Seeking Arrangement or WhatsYourPrice. Here, sugar babies can receive free membership in order to meet wealthy older men and get to know them.

Part of being a sugar baby is remembering that you are a little dose of joy and sexiness in your sugar daddy's life. He already financially supports you, so placing too many emotional demands on him may drive him away. Be open to his requests and be generous with your time. Money, after all, does not grow on trees, and if your sugar daddy does not feel as though you are holding up your end of the relationship, he will not hesitate to move on and choose from the many other young women who would be happy to take your place.

Challenge Round: The Man Who Is Already Attached

So, you meet this amazing, cute guy. He's funny, attractive, smart, kind, and...he already has a girlfriend or a wife. Not fun. What may be a little exciting, though, is seeing whether you can sway your guy away from his current partner and toward yourself. This may seem cunning and dirty, but honestly, it's his own problem, and his relationship with his girlfriend is one that he could leave for someone else.

The first step of getting Mr. Taken is to get his eye wandering. Before anything else, men fall for looks. This means you need to look your best around him. Look sexy and enticing. Chances are, his girlfriend has stopped putting effort to look her most fabulous around him, and he'll appreciate the view. Some new eye candy will make him start wondering about you and getting more curious. This is only the first step, though. A man can enjoy a pretty face and want to sleep with the girl who has it, but physical attraction alone is not enough to make your crush stray from his girl and fall for you.

Looking your best, start to drop hints that you're

interested in him. Maybe throw him a few glances and lock eyes with him. Put on your best "come hither" expression without saying much of a word. This may not get him to come over to you all of a sudden, but it plants the thought of you in his mind. He'll start to wonder if you're into him, and the attention will certainly be a nice ego boost for him. Once he has caught you staring, pull back a little bit for a few days. Soon, he'll be the one staring at you, trying to see if you'll return his gaze. Do look back at him, but don't gaze back. He'll get annoyed that you're not giving him the attention he wants and become even more motivated to make you notice him. Once you've gotten into his head, start flirting with his friends a teensy bit. The little man-squad will start talking about you, and the fact that they are all acquainted with you will inspire some friendly competition among the lads. When your crush realizes that you talk to his friends, he will feel the need to "win out" over them somehow. He'll definitely make more of an effort to impress you if he gets even an inkling that he's being compared to his friends by an attractive woman.

This next portion of the process of getting a guy to leave his girlfriend may sound a little devious, but it's essential. To zero in, you need to understand what her strengths and weaknesses are—what do your crush and his girlfriend disagree on? What are some flaws about her that may get to him sometimes? Look at her social media, friend group, or anywhere to figure out this information. Use it to your advantage by bringing up similar issues with your crush and compare preferences and personal issues. This step will make him wonder whether he should be with you instead of his current girlfriend.

In general, make sure you guys have great conversations. Your crush should feel as if he can tell you anything, maybe even some secrets he wouldn't even tell his girlfriend. By building deep rapport with him, you are laying a foundation of emotional intimacy. A guy will not leave his girlfriend for someone who is not equal to or better than her. Offer your fun company, shoulder to cry on, and emotional intimacy to continue to make him wonder if maybe you should be his girlfriend. This is also where flirting becomes important. Don't be too forward about this by doing something like sending him a late-night text or asking him out, though. Instead, be shy and coy. He should get a little bit confused and ask himself if you're flirting with him or if he's the one giving you all the attention. I can't stress enough, however, how important it is to flirt subtly. The goal is to seem mysterious and continue to convey the possibility of attraction, so he thinks his blossoming little crush on you was his idea.

Once he's receptive to your flirting game, it's time to kick it up a notch. Introduce some nice, girly touches into the mix. Lightly touch his arm when you laugh or tell him he has something in his hair and offer to remove it. Getting into his personal space, even in a way that isn't overtly sexual, still builds the chemistry between you two. Experiencing chemistry with the object of your affections continues the process of orienting him away from his girlfriend and toward yourself.

Eventually, start hinting that you like him. If he's broken up with his girlfriend and the flirting is reciprocal and consistent, go for it and tell him you have more than "just friends" on your mind. If he hasn't broken up with his girlfriend, start to act like his girlfriend. Ask him to hang out alone in situations that may be a date, but not so romantic that you could not talk your way out of questions about the status of your relationship to this man. Throw some late-night phone calls into the mix, too. As I said, start taking up some responsibilities normally reserved for a romantic partner.

Once you've done these steps, he should be thinking seriously about leaving his girlfriend for you. You've planted the seed in his mind and shown him your best self—what he's missing out on if he stays with his current girlfriend.

Chapter 4: How to Flirt Like the High School Gal Pal You Were Always Jealous Of

"Choose, tease, ignore, and catch." We're moving on to step number two now, the teasing phase. This is arguably the most important step in the process of getting the guy you want. Teasing and flirting with a guy is absolutely an art form. It requires nuance, subtlety, and most of all, confidence.

The flirting game proves that men are mere mortals at the mercy of us women. Knowing this, the way to his heart may actually be through his weaknesses. All men are suckers for certain moves, and they also have some personal variation in what they find absolutely irresistible. The key to playing on his weaknesses is to intrigue him. It's a combination of simply what he finds sexy and what he perceives as qualities he wants in a woman that he himself does not possess.

What Can't He Resist: Some of Men's Most Common Weaknesses

A few of most men's weaknesses are as follows: physical desire, confidence, mystery, and vulnerability. Physical desire is a huge category, but it basically covers appearance and physical touch. With respect to the kinds of looks that men find attractive, it isn't all about breasts and legs. While a tight dress can certainly make a man double take, it is not what totally teases him. The first irresistible move you can pull is with your face, not your body. It's called the Tilt and Gaze. It requires you to catch his gaze while looking up with your head slightly tilted. It's cute and curious looking, making him want to protect you, but it's also a little bit suggestive. He can't help but wonder if you're interested when your eyes meet his and gaze ever-so-slightly longingly.

Men also find displays of your femininity attractive, like talking in a tiny baby voice or being clingy—nothing too over-the-top but just a little reminder of how flattering you may be to his masculinity. A good way to play up your womanhood lies a lot in appearance. Think sexy and comfy fabrics like cashmere, satin, and lace. These fabrics are girly and irresistibly touchable, especially if they show a little skin. Think of snuggly, deep V-neck sweaters, and lace camisoles to show off your sexy shoulders. Women are generally more tactile than men; we have softer skin, longer hair (usually), and soft curves. Use these to your advantage to get him thinking about running his hands all over you.

The next part of preying on his weaknesses of the flesh is to smell delicious always. Having a good smell actually goes a long way with men. A woman with hair that smells like shampoo and fresh scent sticks in his mind. The scent is the human sense most connected to emotion and long-term memory. By having a delicious signature scent, he'll be sure to associate those smells with your presence.

The next set of all men's weaknesses are way more than skin deep. Confidence and mystery are so sexy to men because they show a man you're a high-value woman he'll have to work for. Most men love a little bit of a chase, and when confronted with a challenge, you can imagine how satisfying it will be to get their way. Self-confidence is so attractive because it is so positive and refreshing to be around. The confident woman generally has a good attitude and is fun to be around. She knows herself pretty well and seems to like what she knows quite a bit. It's only natural then that a man sees this and sees that there must be some great qualities in this woman. Self-confidence is also accepting and compassionate. Someone who believes in themselves never feels the need to tear someone down or test someone's loyalty. This person is accepting of others because she is accepting of herself.

Self-assuredness, most attractively, conveys

power and agency. A woman who knows who she is and what she wants is not wishy-washy or mousy. Men can't help but want to know this woman because she goes after what she wants and is not afraid of speaking her mind and being her total self. Men also know that self-confident women are generally more fun sexual partners—they know sexual desire is nothing to be ashamed of and aren't afraid to let loose. Every guy wants to sleep with a woman like this and capture her.

Mystery serves a similar role as a man's weakness to confidence. When a woman is ever so slightly mysterious, if she has lots of cool hobbies he doesn't know about and seems like she knows something the rest of us don't, the man wants to become her special boy. Mystery traps a man because it makes him want desperately to be her confidante. He thinks that if a woman seems to be hiding a little something mischievous from the whole world, it must be great. Therefore, he will become invested in working toward getting into the mysterious lady's inner world and finding out her little secrets.

Last but not least, vulnerability is also undeniably appealing to most men. Why? It goes back to femininity and humanity. On a surface level, it appeals to men because it plays up femininity. Many men are constantly suppressing their emotions, making sure never to appear sad or hurt. In contrast to that is women's gift of being more in touch with the emotional realm and having the ability to convey them more effectively. If you show a little bit of vulnerability, don't be surprised if he, too, opens up and shares his feelings. Seeing you in a vulnerable moment will make him want to match you in emotion and view you as a beacon of emotional relief.

These are the most general weaknesses most guys have, but all men are individuals. Some of the real progress gets made when you figure out what he personally finds tempting in a woman. Playing on the weaknesses particular to him can entice and allure him. To do this, find out what they are. Maybe he's a sucker for a woman's laugh because he isn't very emotive himself. Maybe he can't get enough of an athletic woman. Perhaps he's just a teensy bit insecure and absolutely needs an ego boost. Once you know what his weakness is, it's time to play.

A great trick is to tease him lightly. Don't poke fun at a topic he's extremely sensitive about, but choose something light and flirty to make a little joke about. If he follows a strict diet out of concern for his physique, it may be cute to say something like, "You still eating all those greens, Popeye?" The whole idea is to get him to laugh a little bit but also get him a little defensive. He'll realize you've been paying attention to him enough to notice little things about him, like his meticulous routines or penchant for a hair product.

Another part of preying on his personal weaknesses is to get his blood flowing. If he's a sucker for the color red on a woman, by all means, wear a daring red dress to happy hour with him. He will see that you possess qualities he finds tempting in a woman and finds himself obsessing over what's so perfect about you. The whole idea is to make yourself a prize just out of his reach.

The Time and Place for Everything

Knowing how to flirt is great, but it can happen everywhere. Not all moves are appropriate for all places. The tricks you can use to snag that office hottie may not be so effective at a bar or a birthday party. The best flirts keep not only the audience in mind but also the setting.

Let's start at the very beginning of your day—your morning iced coffee at the local café. In some ways, this is a great place to flirt because it's low stakes (no one is going home with anyone) and because most people are not expecting to be approached by a friendly and cute stranger such as yourself. It can be a little bit difficult, though, because people often seem to be in a rush at a coffee shop and may seem like they do not want to be approached. Even we might feel a little bit strange approaching someone in a place not normally associated with flirtation. It's pretty likely, though, that you'll spot someone you fancy in a coffee shop. People go in and out of them all the time, after all, so eventually, you will see a guy you wish you know how to strike up a conversation with while on your morning run.

The first step here is to look presentable. I know it's Saturday morning, and you want to go in your pajamas and that you don't normally go out with messy hair and unbrushed teeth, but it's especially important not to do this if you think you may find Mr. Right while getting a cup of coffee. He will not be so excited by your approach if you look like you just rolled out of bed.

Now that you have the look down, it's time to make your move on Joe and his cup of joe. It sounds cheesy, but ask him if he knows any good drinks on the menu with a big smile on your face and lots of eye contact. It'll show him that you're friendly, and it's an easy way to continue the conversation. If it's a weekday, it also helps to ask if he works nearby after asking what he ordered. When he answers you, get excited to know about his job, and take the opportunity to introduce yourself by name and explain whether you live or work around the coffee shop. Easy and friendly conversation topics at a coffee shop work well because he is most likely not looking to go home with you from such a place. Here, going full-on sex kitten may not work. The sexiest thing you can do here is to become flirty, friendly, and interesting.

After you get your coffee, you may see another sexy stud at work, which is tricky because you're at work, where flirting may sometimes be seen as a faux pas. The key to making this work is to have a connection. Work is a vital part of adult life. We often hear great or terrible news while we're there and see our coworkers very frequently. Flirting here is a little bit like flirting with a friend. To snag your workplace cutie, build a friendly relationship with him that is not about only workplace matters. If your job is a little bit boring, talk about anything but work with this guy to make yourself his little ray of sunshine over his monotonous days.

Another important part of flirting with a coworker is developing inside jokes. Inside jokes are a good way to get some sparks flying because they foster a type of privacy or intimacy between you two. You get to share a little secret unrelated to the other people and tasks associated with your job when you develop an inside joke with someone and get to share some laughs. Have fun with it, and be part of the reason he's happy to go to work in the morning.

Once you guys have good workplace banter going, take the friendship out of the office for a night at the bar. Happy is the place where you can start using more typical flirting techniques that would normally not be appropriate at the office. This is where you can poke a little fun at him or touch him on the forearm to emphasize a point. Showing your coworker crush what you're like outside of work gives him a fun glimpse into your life as a whole. It establishes you as a true friend and possible romantic process when you go out and do fun activities with him. Keep the intrigue and hanging out going, and you'll have yourself a professional boo in no time.

The next place you may find a potential man is out having fun on a Friday night at a bar, club, or party. Next time you're out and getting your party on, try flashing him a smile from across the room and give him a wave of your hand and a come hither motion. It makes it immediately obvious that you're interested in him, but you also have to make it seem that he had an equal part in approaching you because he had to respond to your gesture to come over and strike up a conversation.

Approaching a guy at a bar can be scary, so remember K.I.S.S.: Keep It Simple, Stupid. A good opener is simply walking over and saying, "Hi, I'm [so-and-so]. How are you?" This isn't even a trick. It's just a friendly way to approach someone and strike up a conversation. It's also pretty ballsy because it makes it clear you're interested. This is a good thing, though—people are often at bars and parties hoping to meet someone to flirt with and potentially find romance. Being the woman who makes a forward first move will make you stand out and seem confident and fun. Another strategy for making conversation with the cutie ordering a beer is by sitting next to him and complimenting his taste in booze or his outfit. This strategy hits two birds with one stone because he gets a compliment to boost his confidence and because you get to talk to him. He will like that you've noticed some small details about him and are confident enough to share your opinion.

If you're a little too shy to approach him from across the room, though, there is still a pretty good method for you to increase the odds that he'll come over and strike up a conversation. It's all in the eyes—from across the room, lock eyes with him, and hold his gaze between the two of you like a precious object. Then, turn on your smolder by giving him a sultry expression. The face you make need not be over-the-top, but it should make him start wondering about you in at least a bit of a PG-13 way. Look away once you're done, and return to the conversation you were having with your squad. About five minutes later, look back at him and smile. This works because the first look establishes you in his field of vision, and the second look makes it clear that the sexy eye contact between you too wasn't an accident. After the smile, there's a pretty good chance he'll make his way over and start chatting you up.

The Tease Knows How to Please

Now that you know the basics of the approach, it's time to know how to tease him. Teasing is the bad-girl cousin of flirting. Flirting is a little coy, a little shy. Teasing, however, is confident, a teensy bit brash, and very much sexy.

The key to teasing is to maintain compassion without crossing into the territory of nastiness. Effective teasing pivots on whether or not all parties know it's all in good fun. As the teaser, do not employ this tactic with the intent to cut down your crush's self-esteem. He should know that you respect him and enjoy his company but are having a little fun at his expense in order to express romantic interest. Before getting into a specific technique, going over some basic principles of teasing your guy is imperative. Successful teasing can get the wheels turning to make him fall for you, but lousy teasing can alienate him and cause him to avoid you. All effective teasing has a few qualities in common, so a sturdy set of ground rules can set the stage for some productive flirting.

Because teasing is supposed to be a little bit edgy but still friendly, avoid teasing your love interest about qualities he can't change or that he's insecure about. If he's bald and insecure about that, do not incorporate that into your little jokes. In general, avoid topics of pain. If he came from a poor background or feels insecure about a stereotype related to his culture, do not make those the topic of the tease. Teasing your crush about sensitive topics treads into the territory of meanness. Another bad timing for your tease is when he's opening up and being vulnerable. Men often already have extreme difficulty sharing their emotions and being vulnerable, so, dear God, don't make it any harder for him. Teasing him, or even flirting, while he is deeply emotional may cause him not to open up to you again for fear that you won't take him seriously.

As I said, teasing is supposed to be funny. So, do

tease him in a way that plays up how cool you think he is. For example, if he tells you he picked up an extremely hard project at work, make a little joke and say, "Wow...is that because you're sucking up for a promotion?" with a big smile on your face (maybe even touch his shoulder if you're feeling a little daring). Use a little sarcasm when you tease him, too. It should be obvious that you are just playing with him.

In the same category as teasing is flirting. All good teasing is flirting, but not all flirting is teasing. Flirting, in general, is a manner of interaction to demonstrate your sexual or romantic interest in a man. I know that sounds technical and creepy, but a little reminder of the definition of flirting may be helpful. We often go about it, acting as though this one little exchange alone determines our value as women and who we marry. It doesn't. Flirting is meant to be fun for everyone involved with the objective of an outcome where everyone wins.

We already know eye contact and smiles are good, but some more specific techniques are appropriate here. One of the easiest ways to entice while still holding yourself out of reach is to whisper in his ear to tell him something. It doesn't matter whether what you have to say is actually a secret. What counts is that your mouth will be very close to such a sensitive spot on his body, and he'll begin wondering what it's like to be even closer to you. Bonus points if your lips accidentally graze the shell of his ear briefly. Speaking of speech, don't be afraid to throw him some compliments. Men are not used to getting them, and he will begin to associate you with the positive feeling he gets when you tell him sweet things about himself.

If you want to be more bold and sexual, though, you'll have to up your game a little bit. A bold statement would be to place a hand on his cheek or jaw while complimenting him or thanking him for doing you a favor. The venture into his personal space, and the sweet and intimate gesture will make him want to keep working hard to impress you. Another, more forward move is to talk about something romantic and sexy with him, sounding dreamy and soft while you're at it. Wait for a little silence, look him in the eye, and ask, "Are you looking at me like you want to kiss me?" Essentially, this invites him to lean in and plant one on you, even if he's nervous about doing it.

The most aggressive moves usually involve some physical touch, and if you're already pretty sure he's interested, try some of these out. Next time you're talking to him, place a hand on his thigh and slowly move it a little closer to his crotch without actually touching it. This fiery hot trick says one thing: "I want you." Don't be surprised if he jumps you right then and there. Another way to get very close to his personal space is by kissing him on the cheek as you say goodbye, but dangerously close to his lips. Combined with a loooong hug, he'll be wishing you had gone straight for his lips.

Texting Tease

Now that we all have cellular devices and social media, knowing how to extend flirting into the digital realm is indispensable. Flirting over text is easiest at night and when your crush is not busy with pressing obligations. You want to catch him while he's not too busy, and the communication can get steamy, fun, and fast-paced.

One of the easiest ways to flirt over text is to ask a fairly intimate question. In the middle of a conversation, ask him, "what color are your sheets?" or "What do you wear when you sleep?" Although both questions seem fairly innocuous, they are actually pretty loaded with intimacy. The flirty questions you ask over text should generally be somewhat personal and be able to lead into something a little bit sexier. The question about what he wears when he sleeps, for example, can prompt him to answer, "Nothing." If it's late at night, and he says he's laying in bed, you can respond, "Hm...I wish I were there."

Another classic way to get him hot is to send him a sexy snapchat where you show plenty of cleavage. It does not need to have any kind of overtly sexual caption or show off any serious nudity, but show enough breast to make the picture just a bit risqué. This move is a bit interesting because, while he may not respond by directly mentioning your little display, he may be a bit flirtatious the next time you guys text or see him in person. Part of the point of teasing him over text message is that it builds temptation. It does not happen in person, so any sexy ideas you plant in his mind are largely a product of your man's own imagination responding to your suggestions.

Another avenue to take advantage of is Instagram. Instagram is great for giving flirty compliments because men are likely to make themselves look attractive or show off a cool activity they are doing on this platform. Next time he posts a shirtless vacation picture, don't be scared to message him privately and say, "Holy crap, you must be working out hard. Your arms look insane!" Instagram makes it easy to give compliments because people are already fishing for them there. He will enjoy the ego boost and know you are flirting by complimenting his looks.

Texting is all about the suggestion, which makes it the ultimate teasing tool. If you want to text your crush during the day, say, "I had a dream about you last night; it was so weird!" Then, describe a dream where you guys kissed or had a sexual encounter. He'll be flattered he made his way into your dreams, and you guys will have a great excuse to continue talking about sex.

Smartphones, computers, Facebook, Instagram, Snapchat, and Twitter are all fabulous tools at your disposal to flirt with your dude of choice. When in doubt, remember that the whole point is to have fun with it and play a little head game with him to start imagining doing some dirty things with you. Take advantage of the fact that everything you say over text is up for interpretation—saying that you're laying in bed feeling very hot will go a very long way in getting him to picture you sweating in bed with him. For digital flirtation, less is more.

How Men Fall in Love

You've done all your flirting, gone on a few dates, maybe you've hooked up, but you don't know where the relationship is going yet and how your new squeeze really feels about you. This is probably the most stressful part of dating because a mismatch in commitment and interest has the potential to hurt our feelings and devastate us. There are seven steps to getting a man to fall in love with you. Know how to play each one, so you wind up with the man of your dreams.

1. **Physical Attraction.** This is the first and shallowest stage of falling in love. It's the movie moment where he checks you out from across the room while you're standing around with your friends, and you guys lock eyes for an extended period. Okay, it doesn't always happen like that, but you get the idea. Regardless of how it actually happens, this is the stage where a guy first decides whether

he finds you sexually attractive.

The best way to manipulate this step is to look your best and use open body language. This means keeping your shoulders back and arms away from your torso while you talk to him. Appear to look friendly and open to conversation. The physical attraction phase is where a smoldering gaze will do you a great deal of good to express your interest in him and getting him to want to be in your personal space.

This step is extremely important but only because it's the first one. In other words, getting him to fall for you is not solely dependent on your crush finding you beautiful. You simply need to catch his eye to strike up a flirty conversation and keep on making him find you sexually attractive by wearing cute clothes and taking care of yourself. The next steps are the real meat of the process of falling in love. Men find many women beautiful, but only a few men marry a woman only because she's good-looking. The next steps are where you build a connection and a foundation for the relationship.

2. **The Crush.** This is the phase where a guy starts thinking about you nonstop. He's figured out that he thinks you're easy on the eyes and that he's physically attracted to you,

but now, he can't get you off his mind. He doesn't necessarily love you at this point, but he certainly wants to be around you and enjoys your company. This is the step where a man often asks a woman out.

To make sure this step goes smoothly, be open to his advances, and make it clear that you are happy to have your man's attention. Remember, he's not in love with you yet, so if he does not think you're interested or doesn't see a reason to expend any more energy on you, he'll walk away. Some of the signs that he's entered the infatuation phase are texting you very frequently and stealing glances at you. He may be trying to impress you in low stakes ways when he has started crushing on you by bragging a little bit or looking good to see you. Basically, he'll be acting a little bit the way we picture high school crushes.

In this phase, while it's important to be receptive, don't be too desperate. Men love a chase of some kind, so don't ignore him or play hard to get. To make sure he wants to work for you, make yourself a teensy bit unavailable, so he'll continue to have the motivation to get to know you. Do not have sex with him on the first date, and feel free not to answer his texts immediately. Holding yourself just beyond his reach like a delicious food in front of a hungry man (and giving him a little bite occasionally) will keep the chase going and make him want to keep getting to know you.

3. **Attraction.** Now that you've shown some reciprocal interest, he'll let himself feel some more attraction toward you. Guys don't like expending energy on a prospect that may go nowhere, and now that he knows you're open to him, he'll become more invested.

In this stage, rejecting him would upset him or break his heart. He is not exactly in love with you, but he has made some emotional investment in you and wants you to like him back. If you're in this phase, it is possible that he has started to show a little bit of vulnerability around you and open up on more personal topics about himself. Your job in this step is also to show investment and emotional vulnerability. Oversharing and going into sob stories is not necessary, but opening up is appropriate here. During the attraction phase, you and your man begin getting to know each other on a deeper level and the appreciation of your physical appearance from Phase 1 gains an emotional dimension.

4. **Showing Off.** Once you seem receptive to his advances and he seems interested, he'll accelerate his efforts to impress you. He hasn't developed irrevocable romantic

feelings and devotion to you yet, but he's seriously going to be trying to make you interested and impressed.

When he's trying to impress you, he'll start taking you on dates to expensive restaurants and buying you nice gifts. Basically, he wants to show you how great he is. In this phase, keep showing interest, and do what you've been doing in the previous step, showing how much you appreciate his gifts, dates, and consideration.

5. **Persuasion.** This is when a guy starts wondering if you guys may turn serious. I know, it seems late in the game, but it takes men longer than women to become attached to a romantic partner. Here, a guy will be trying to get you to fall in love with him even though he's not so open to giving all of himself yet.

He is undeniably into you and wants to go out with you, but the fear sets in during this phase. He's uncertain about what else he can do to make you like him because the dates and gifts have already happened. Basically, his and your personality and cooperation are the key ingredients in this step. Show off that you are flirty and fun in this stage but that you also have emotional depth and understanding. Now is when he starts wanting to get serious with you, so be sure to deliver the girlfriend package—sexy, sweet, fun, and intelligent.

6. **Security.** When a man establishes security, he thinks he knows that he's gotten you to fall in love with him (whether or not that's true). Knowing that he has your heart, he'll actually start to put in the intellectual effort to decide as to how he feels about you. He has certainly enjoyed your company up to this point and would be sad to lose it, but this is the first time he's said to himself, "Do I actually want to commit to her?"

Right now, the best thing you can do is put no pressure on him. If you put him in the hot seat and try forcing him into commitment, he'll sour on you because you'll seem desperate and clingy. Just bide your time and be the best girlfriend you can be. Keep any fighting or difficulty to a minimum at this point.

7. **Love.** Finally! The last step—he's certain he likes you and wants to invest in you. If he decides he likes you, he'll let himself fall in love and fully open up to you. He'll have no reservations about you and be happy to commit to you. If he's decided he is not into you, he'll start avoiding you and act distant. He'll stop buying you little gifts and doing you favors.

Once he's decided he loves you, though, you don't have much to worry about. Now, you can enjoy the bliss and security of his continued affections.

Okay, Stop

So you've done all the teasing, flirting, and tempting you're supposed to, and he seems hooked. Now, you need to pull back. He needs to work for your affection, and you need to test him to see if he'll reach out when you withhold just a bit. The next chapter will cover this step more completely, so you'll know the proper way to ignore him just a little bit to make him sweat and work for your attention.

☆ If you have gotten this far and have achieved more than you thought possible, please consider leaving a short review for the book on Amazon, it means a lot to me! Thank you.

Chapter 5: Ignore Him

Think about the last time you were unsure of whether a guy likes you. It was beginning to feel as though you were the one constantly initiating conversation and plans with him. You couldn't be sure whether you were just beating him to it or whether he was just not that into you. Perhaps, you didn't know what you could do to know whether he wanted you and how to force him to step up his game. This is where pulling away from the situation could have done you well.

Once you're done teasing and flirting, ignoring him a little bit can be useful because it makes him feel the need to do some work to get you. This phase of making sure you get the guy you want serves to show him just how valuable you are and make him go a little crazy over you.

The Method of Doing Nothing

In case it isn't obvious, the objective of reeling in your contact with your dude is not to give him a silent treatment. It's more of a way to make him realize he misses you just a bit and that you're not just an option for him.

Ignoring him and pulling away can come in many forms, believe it or not. Don't take "ignore" so literally. One way to ignore your man of choice is to simply act a little bit less impressed with him than you did while you were flirting with him. Your dude will sense that something is amiss and feel as though he needs to work even harder to get your attention and praise. In fact, making him work harder is kind of like getting him to make an investment. By upping his game, he's expending more time and energy on you and realizing that there's a chance he could lose you.

Another way to ignore him is to do just that. "Forget" to answer his texts sometimes, or take your sweet time responding. Let the phone ring a few times before picking it up when he calls. The whole idea here is to make a little bit anxious and to make him miss you. In this situation, he's forced to make contact if he wants to hear from you and continue the great thing you two had going during the flirting stage. Don't go one hundred percent on this, though. Be nice and pleasant when you respond to him.

In general, don't be too available. If he asks to

hang out one night, tell him you already have plans. Make him aware that you have a whole exciting life that he is not (yet) included in. Just make him wait for any nice thing from you. If he wants to make plans, tell him, "I can't tonight. Maybe I can on Wednesday, though." Then, wait for him to make contact to follow up with this plan.

Why Does Ignoring Him Work?

Ignoring the guy you're into sounds counterintuitive, but it makes sense. First of all, if he really likes you, he will actually start the chase to get you to act the way you were during the flirtation once again. When he realizes how much he misses your attention and affection, he will be compelled to try getting it back.

There's a bit of an addiction principle going on here—it's a reward system called a variable reward schedule, and it's a powerful psychological principle. Basically, it looks like a bunch of little lab mice pressing a button to get a reward. For the first few trials, the mice get a reward for pushing the button, but eventually, they stop getting their treat for every time they push the button. Sometimes, they will get the reward after pushing the button, say, five times, but other times, it will take ten or fourteen, or some other number of button pushes. The mice do not know when the reward will come, so they press the button practically continuously to get their reward.

A variable reward schedule results in the behavior (pressing the button) repeated the most number of times on any type of reward schedule.

Not to sound creepy, but when you pull away from your man a little bit, he becomes a little bit like the lab rat desperately pushing the button to get his reward. He's gotten used to your affection and flirty behavior during the teasing stage and then when you pull away, he still wants his reward. Like the lab rat who starts pushing the button harder and more frequently when it doesn't know when the next reward is coming, your man will start to try harder and harder to get back into your good graces.

Ignoring a man is effective on a more emotional level because it makes you seem like an unattainable prize. Guys love winning due to their naturally competitive streak. When you cut off some of your acknowledgment of him, he realizes he's in a competition of sorts. He wants to win you back, and he realizes he'll have to work for your attention. Most great guys meet plenty of girls who practically throw themselves at them, so they don't have to work very hard. You acting not very impressed, however, will make you stand out from the crowd. He'll wonder why you don't seem to think he's very special and because he's so used to others behaving as though he is, he will start to go out of his way to wow you and get you to pay attention to him.

This phase also serves you in a way that has nothing to do with making a man like you, and it's actually pretty important for laying a foundation for a relationship. If he seems to take you for granted a little bit, becoming unavailable can kick him into gear and get him to behave properly. Basically, it shows him that you are not to be messed with, ignored, or taken for granted. He will realize that you are not here to screw around and that you demand respect. If he doesn't comply, you know the right thing to do is drop his ass – if he gets better and starts acting like a good boyfriend material, great for you. You've found a guy who actually cares about staying on your good side.

How to Stick to Ignoring Him

Throughout this section, you've probably been sitting around and saying to yourself, "Yeah. Fuck him. I can ignore him!" Then, when he texts you after you're done reading, you will struggle not to respond immediately. Stick to your guns during this phase, though, and read on for tips to keeping yourself just out of reach from him.

When you're trying to ignore someone, act on your pride. Remind yourself that if you reach out, you're giving into your feelings for him. You do not want to sound needy or obsessed with him. The coolest girls know that every guy is replaceable, so act like it.

While you're ignoring him, you may seriously start to miss him. This is only natural—you do like him, after all. Stay busy then. Plan fun activities with your girl squad, work out, and put in some extra hours at work. You don't want to get too bored during the ignoring phase because the loneliness that often accompanies idle hands can lead you straight to your text messages, asking him how he's doing.

Overall, remind yourself that you don't need a man the way you need food and water. You may like this dude a lot or have some feelings for him, but he is ultimately more of decoration in your life than a serious necessity. You are worth way more than chasing after a guy and begging for his attention. Believe it, and act like it.

Time to Move On?

So, how do you know when to stop ignoring him? Ignoring him too little won't teach him anything, but ignoring him too long will make him move on and forget about you. You need to time reintroducing him into your life properly in order to lead him into falling for you successfully.

You'll know when it's time to go back to flirting and validating your man when he reaches back out to you. Basically, he needs to prove he's interested before you start responding to his texts consistently.

Wait for him to demonstrate that he misses you. This can happen in many ways. Maybe, Mr. Man will reach out to hang out or simply start texting you, asking how you are doing or sharing funny cat videos. When he reaches out, and it's time to reel him back in, you'll know because you will get the distinct sensation that he's trying to remind you that he still exists.

When you take him back, though, don't do it all at once. Maybe just start by responding a little bit sooner than you have been but still not immediately. Go back to smiling a little bit more around him and seeming happy to see him. Think of it this way: do not warm up to him immediately after icing him out for a while. Instead, you need to thaw out the relationship a little bit slow to draw out the relief-giving process of giving him your attention again. He can't feel too comfortable too soon. Otherwise, he will think that getting you back was too easy, and he will have learned nothing..

Chapter 6: Going in for the Kill and Catching Him in the End

So we've effectively moved away from ignoring him, and now, he's initiating contact and making it clear that he actually likes you. Now, it's time to get him to fall for you and want to commit. I'm not going to lie to you—this step can be a little bit stressful and emotionally exhausting, but it's obviously worth it to snatch up the man of your dreams.

To get him to commit to you, you need to get him to fall fully for you. In the previous three stages, he's certainly liked you and appreciated you but has not fallen totally in love with you. His emotions are not yet tied up with you, and, frankly, he can walk away if he wants right now and be over you pretty quickly. We want to correct this and make him crave your presence in his life as a consistent source of affection and love.

Step 1: Make Him Fall for You

The first step to making him fall for you is to stay positive. I know this sounds cheesy, but do not let your fear of rejection or pain affect your behavior or self-esteem. This isn't important because it's warm and fuzzy, and I'm trying to build up your confidence. It's important because if you let yourself fall into a negative head space, it will show. The man you've chosen, teased, and ignored will not fall for you if he feels like you're cynical. Commit yourself to be a positive force. You don't necessarily have to indulge all of your feelings for him, but that does not mean you have to continue being cold toward him. The ignoring phase is over baby; no need to keep being cold.

This phase is where you give him a sample of the whole package. It's when you listen to him spill his feelings while also being sexy, smart, down to hang out, etc. While women fall for a man knowing his flaws, men can be a little bit silly and feel as though the women they fall for need to be indispensable to their own happiness. Therefore, make yourself a non-negotiable necessity in his life. Find out what his other relationships have lacked, and give these things to him. Give him a taste of the stable, loving girlfriend he wants but without giving him everything just yet.

When you're showing yourself to be exactly what he needs, don't give him everything. This means hearing him out and doing more listening than speaking but also making sure to have plans outside of him. If you're busy, then tell him. Basically, don't make too much time for him or let him suck up too much energy. Remind yourself that if your man wants boyfriend privileges, he has to put in boyfriend work and take boyfriend responsibilities. Giving too much too quickly is why so many relationships never materialize. Why would he buy the cow if he can get the milk for free?

In the same vein of only giving him a sample, do not be too possessive of him or act like you need him for anything. Show that you like his company, but coming off as possessive is a huge turnoff. It makes him anxious that a relationship with you would be full of fighting and reassuring you that he's actually into you. Remember the first few chapters of this book? Desperation is straight up unattractive. On the flip side, independence and having your life together are.

Honesty and authenticity also go a long way in getting a guy to fall for you. Emotional intimacy is what separates a guy thinking you're a fun hookup from a guy thinking he wants you in his life consistently. When you behave as your true self, you give him a taste of what is to come from a relationship with you. Maybe it's your amazing sense of humor, your compassion, your penchant for physical affection—whatever it is that makes you show it off. By this point, a man will be able to tell if you seem fake or pretending to be someone you're not. Be honest with him about yourself. Set a standard for what you want with him. You may not have to tell him directly that you want a relationship, but make it clear that there is a standard he needs to meet if he wants to continue seeing you. In a past relationship, I once told a man what I said before: "I can't give you boyfriend privileges if you don't want to take any boyfriend responsibilities or put in boyfriend work." If he walks, then you could have been doing better the whole time, but if he stays, then you've found yourself a man you can work with. Honesty works for you regardless of whether or not your man chooses to stick around because either you dodge a bullet if he abandons ship in the face of accountability or you find a man who is willing to prove that he wants you.

What is one way to withhold boyfriend privileges? Don't have sex with him, or if you do choose to have sex with him, withhold cuddles and sleepovers until he commits or expresses some feelings for you. I know it sounds old-fashioned, but taking things slow with a new boyfriend can be healthy for both of you. By keeping physical intimacy at bay, you can avoid feeling hurt and used if he turns out to disappoint you. On his end, not getting any from you can shift his focus toward getting to know you as a person and allowing his positive feelings toward you to grow. When two people have sex too soon, they often lose motivation to keep getting to know each other and no longer feel the need to impress each other. And why should a man want to keep getting to know all of your amazing qualities if gets what he wants without any commitment? If you employ this strategy and he keeps wanting to get to know you, be fairly certain that he definitely likes you and that if he keeps getting to know you, he will probably like you enough to wind up committing to you.

Another way to get him to fall in love is to keep being as sexy and fun as you were at the beginning of the relationship. When two people begin getting comfortable, one person usually drops off their effort at presenting their best selves. Don't stop dolling yourself up to see him, and do not stop being a fun burst of energy in his life. Show that you are the gift that keeps on giving. Continue to be friendly toward his friends and act enthusiastic about whatever is going on in his life. You want to continue being a leading lady. Remember: show him what you're like as girlfriend material. If you've started sleeping with your man by this phase, let him know how lucky you feel that you get to see him naked. Stay starry-eyed, and do your best to continue the honeymoon feeling of endless romance and exploration that men crave in a woman.

Get Him to Actually Commit

Ugh, I know! He's fallen for you, he likes you a lot, he goes out of his way for you—but he has said nothing in the way of exclusivity or commitment. I can only imagine how frustrated you are, wondering if he's behaving toward other women the same way he behaves toward you.

Imagine attraction and investment like two levers in your personal control room. You have probably made a mistake before of feeling some attraction to someone, so the attraction lever gets pulled even a little bit. In response to feeling your attraction lever move, you may have pulled down hard on the investment lever and given a guy a ton of your time and generosity at even the slightest bit of attraction. Don't do that ever again. To get him to commit to you, pull your investment lever down carefully and temperately. Basically, only match him in his investment. If you show a little bit of investment and he doesn't reciprocate it, pull back a little bit. Not only is showing too much commitment too quickly going to scare him away, but it shows him that he doesn't have to put in too much work to get you. Make him work, sis! Imagine yourself on a path with the man you want—walk right next to him instead of walking in front of him and dragging him along with you by his ankles.

To get him to commit, you need to do what you did to get him to fall for you: make yourself indispensable. Rock his world. A man will not commit to you out of a sense of duty or morality. You need to change his world to make him want to keep you in it. You gotta bring the sex, the fun, the intelligent conversation, and the emotion—all while remaining ever-so-slightly unavailable. Make it clear to him, too. Do not go too far out of your way for him too frequently before he commits. Do not introduce him to family or friends until he commits.

Getting him to commit is all about seeming like the full package that he has to earn. Independence and demonstrated self-assuredness will do you wonders to make him want to spend more time with you and stop looking around toward other women.

Common Mistakes in the Catching Phase and How to Avoid Them

These instructions sound too simple, right? Often, it's helpful to know what not to do and trust that everything will work out as long as you keep him coming back for more. When deciding when to commit to a girl, a man can be especially critical of her. He'll say things to himself like, "I really don't like that she doesn't seem interested in my hobby, so it'll never work," or, "I just feel like...she's kind of insecure? I can't be with someone who constantly needs me to call her beautiful." Meanwhile, you're making all of these mistakes without even realizing it sometimes because it seems like there's nothing more you can do after the ignoring phase. WRONG! Steer clear of the actions described in this portion of the chapter to make your love life a little bit easier.

One of the most common mistakes is pushing for promises. During the first time you have sex, do not finish, and immediately ask him, "what are we?" If he feels pressure to make a decision too quickly, his decision will be to leave you. I know how bad the uncertainty of where a relationship is going may feel, but just go with the flow. Instead of obsessing over the actual catch, focus more on simply having fun with this guy.

Honesty is also key. If he says from the get-go that he is not looking for commitment, believe him. So many women make the mistake of believing that they can chase and beg a man into submission, but see the previous point for why this does not work. Chasing him and giving him too much simply sends the message that you're the kind of woman who can be walked all over. Objectively speaking, it's pathetic, and from his perspective, you simply seem as if you're a source of free sex and affection.

The mentality you should have when you want him to commit is to commit yourself to the process of relationships, not to the outcome. When you commit yourself to get a man to commit without appreciating the whole process, you lose sight of the fact that you are getting to know someone. In other words, you shouldn't commit to him too early. Frequently, we are so wrapped up in how cute a guy is or how fun we have with him that we miss some serious red flags about him and maybe even about ourselves. Allowing the relationship to take a natural course will take the pressure off both of you and ensure that you are getting to know him through the process described in this book.

Chapter 7: Keeping Your Man Once You've Snatched Him

Congratulations on snagging your sexy, new boy toy! You followed all the steps, and he finally fell for you and made a commitment to exclusivity with you. I couldn't be more happy for you. Relationships take work, though, and they often fail before they ever reach their true potential. Both men and women often stop putting in the effort as soon as their new partner expresses a desire to stick around. Do not be this person. The same way you would become annoyed if a friend became boring and inconsiderate as soon as you call them "best friend," a man will regret settling down with you if you don't continue to cultivate yourself and the relationship. He has invested in you by agreeing to enter into a relationship, so make an effort to show him that was a great choice on his part.

To keep him with you, continue to work on yourself even though he already thinks you're great enough to be in a relationship with him.

Relationships are about two people growing together and teaching each other about love and life. The same way you want to be with someone ambitious and hardworking, your man wants the same. Showing investment in a relationship is showing investment in yourself. This will mean challenging yourself not to be petty during an argument. For some women, it will take the form of standing up for themselves and their ideals. Basically, don't assume that your life is complete just because you've found your dream guy. Relationships are great, but time and responsibility do not simply cease to matter because someone loves you. Keep working on yourself, and set an example to inspire your man to do the same.

Something else I see all the time is a woman who puts on makeup every single day, wears cute outfits when seeing her crush, and goes to the gym consistently to stay in great shape. Once a guy commits to her, though, she does a total one-eighty. She gains fifteen pounds and starts hanging out in sweatpants. I hate to break it to you, but looks still matter even though he has invested in you. You know how people sell a stock when its value goes down. The initial investment they made by purchasing it doesn't mean that they'll keep it when it goes back because they are somehow emotionally attached to it. The same goes for you. Do not get so comfortable and relaxed that looking sloppy or less than great becomes the norm. He most likely became interested in you for your looks, initially. That will not change, no matter how much he loves you.

Also, do not let the fun fall off just because the relationship has gotten serious. Extend the honeymoon phase by having sex with him enthusiastically and always showing that you are attracted to him physically. Continue to go out on dates to fun places like you did during the initial dating process. Your boyfriend started dating you because of what you showed him before he decided he was done looking for a woman, and he hopes that you'll continue to do all those great things (and more) now that you are in a relationship.

The security of a relationship should actually give you comfort in trying new things with your man to keep it fresh and exciting. Try some new sex positions or some kinky handcuffs, for instance. Maybe go skydiving and have a bonding experience of what feels like near-death. Experiencing new things together is part of what it means for you and your man to grow together and learn from each other.

Show Him Your Love

Once you are in a relationship, show your boo how much you appreciate and love him. It's honestly the gift that keeps on giving. When you show him you love him when he does something nice, he will enjoy the praise and be more likely to repeat that behavior in the future. Showing that you love him also shows him how committed you are to the relationship and make him feel so warm and fuzzy about you that he'll practically become addicted to how sweet you can be.

The best way to show someone you love them in the simplest way is to demonstrate that this person is a priority. While sitting on the couch, talking with your boyfriend and the phone rings, do not interrupt the conversation to answer the call, unless it's important. It'll show him that you are present with him and reinforce that you care what he has to say. He will feel good about the fact that you don't take his presence for granted. Romantic relationships also require respect. This means that while you can call him out on crappy behavior or mistakes, it should be well-intentioned, constructive criticism— not nitpicking and obsessing over his flaws. Let your man know that you love and accept him just the way he is. If it's something you would not criticize a friend for, maybe you ought not to bring it up to a boyfriend either.

Another way to show him you love him is to engage in intimate, romantic activities together. No, I don't just mean sex, although some of your activities may find your way into the realm of eroticism—I mean simple gestures and activities that you would not normally do with someone else. Go stargazing or watch the sunset and admire the sky together. It can be quite a spiritual experience with the right person. Plan a romantic night in with wine, candles, and the works. Showing him that you want to put in the effort will go a long way. He'll consider you the best girlfriend ever if you cook him his favorite dinner at the end of a long week or on his birthday.

Show him you love him through respect or cooperation. Build him up and support him, even when you are angry or hurt. Arguments happen in every relationship, but don't play dirty. Do not compare him to your ex or tell him you could have done better in the dating department. You can point out when he has done something wrong, but don't bring up past mistakes in an argument about something else or attack his character. Not only it does not show that you love him, but it also shows a pretty nasty side of you. Do not be your worst self around your partner. Communicate your ideas calmly and directly. Remind yourself that you love this man when you are angry, and it will show in the compassion and forgiveness you display by working with him toward solutions to conflicts.

Keep it Fresh!

No matter how kind and compassionate both partners in a relationship may be, sometimes the boredom sets in and leads to one partner growing a little bit dissatisfied. If the relationship becomes dull, your man may begin wishing he could go back to the single life—chasing girls, drinking with the boys, and not worrying about anyone. This is preventable, though! Keep your man on his toes, and he won't feel the need to stray or crave a return to bachelorhood.

One of the easiest ways to do this is by keeping the romance and heat alive. Send your guy a sexy text while he's at work every now and then, and make him get ready for a steamy night. Initiate sex frequently and show your wild side. Many men fear that in a long-term relationship, they are giving up sexual novelty and excitement. Prove him wrong, and invest in sexy lingerie; buy massage oils and candles and try some kinky fantasies you two share. Continuing to develop your sex life will serve to bond you guys through shared experience and will also keep him coming back for more of you.

Another way to keep a relationship exciting is by setting goals together. It could be anything from getting healthy and committing yourselves to clean eating and gym attendance, but it could also be a commitment to saving money for your future together. It sounds counterintuitive, but creating goals together will remind both of you that you're in it together. You will share failures, victories, elation, sorrow, and everything in between Creating goals that you guys can share will increase the investment both of you have in each other and will foster constant growth and improvement.

Vacations are also good for relationships. If both of you save up and take a vacation from work at the same time, a beach vacation can do quite a bit of good. You guys will get to share a fabulous break from life together and just focus on each other, having fun in a new place. Think of it—sightseeing, food, sex, beaches! A vacation gives both of you the gift of each other. Sometimes, some undivided attention is just what a relationship needs to ensure that you guys don't get too caught up in the trials and tribulations of life.

My personal favorite, a quick pick-me-up, is playing a board game and ordering a pizza. Board games are fun, competitive, and free (if you already own a couple). Playing a board game together every now and then can bring out your silly and creative side. Watching your man get all flustered over a wrong move can be adorable, and he will enjoy watching you get feisty while you score points. You can even make it a sexy board game or card game, like strip poker. Combining sex, jokes, and some friendly competition can be a hot time for you guys. It serves to remind him that you really are the whole package.

Last But Not Least, Go Back to the Beginning

We had a whole chapter on insecurity at the beginning of this book, but it's always relevant, in my opinion. Insecurity is a relationship destroyer. It can cause partners to become clingy, argumentative, suspicious, unfaithful, and mean; it can create a whole host of other problems. You can't expect a man to have any faith in you if you have none in yourself.

To avoid relationship insecurity, you may need to do some serious soul searching. It'll be hard; you may have to revisit some painful memories of ex-boyfriends, high school bullies, a troubled parent, or maybe a different kind of trauma in your past. It will pay off, though. If you do not feel secure in a relationship, you simply cannot feel happy in it because you are more focused on losing it than enjoying it.

To start, work on your self-esteem and remind yourself that you are great. This step actually does not require your man to do anything. Start a new hobby and take care of yourself. Maybe you feel bad that you are a smoker, so attempt to quit it. Building your self-esteem and proving to yourself that you are worthy will help quell your fears that your man will cheat on you or abandon you.

You need to let go of your upsetting past experiences. It can be easy to let painful memories of the past inform how you feel in your new relationships, but work on letting them go. Talk to your man about what happened to you in the past and be open with him. He will appreciate the honesty and be glad that your insecurity does not come from a shady place. If you think you may need professional help getting over your low self-confidence, therapy can be the best investment you ever make for your happiness.

Now that you've gotten to how to have a healthy, happy relationship, you're good to go. You chose the right man, teased him into interest, ignored him to show him who's boss, and finally got him to settle down with you. Go on and be merry. You're well-prepared to find satisfying relationships with great men and show off how great you are.

Conclusion

Thanks for making it through to the end of the book, let's hope it was informative and able to provide you with all of the tools you need to achieve your goals, whatever it is that they may be. Just because you've finished this book doesn't mean there is nothing left to learn on the topic, and expanding your horizons is the only way to find the mastery you seek.

Now that you have made it to the end of this book, you hopefully have an understanding of how to get started attracting the man of your dreams, as well as a strategy or two, or three, that you are anxious to try for the first time. Before you go ahead and start giving it your all, however, it is important that you have realistic expectations as to the level of success you should expect in the near future.

While it is perfectly true that some people experience serious success right out of the gate, it is an unfortunate fact of life that they are the exception rather than the rule. What this means is that you should expect to experience something of a learning curve, especially when you are first figuring out what works for you. This is perfectly normal, however, and if you persevere you will come out the other side better because of it. Instead of getting your hopes up to an unrealistic degree, you should think of your time spent finding the right man as a marathon rather than a sprint which means that slow and steady will win the race every single time.

Finally, if you found this book useful in anyway, a review on Amazon is always appreciated!

I hope that this book has helped you to catch the love of your life. If you enjoyed this reading please leave a short review on Amazon. Thank you!

OTHER BOOKS FROM THE AUTHOR

How to Get Your Ex Back

The 4 Weeks Foolproof Program to Assess Yourself, Get Him Crawl Back to You and Keep the Fire Burning

https://www.amazon.com/dp/B07T8JWR5K

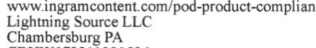